## WHAT PEOPLE ARE SAYING

"New way to look at a difficult subject."

"Liked the relevance to all aspects of shame."

"Practical and easy to interpret."

"Kristina's writing is incredible, easy to understand and leaves you feeling empowered."

"I have a new tool to help me in life."

"From the heart and practical."

"You've changed my life!"

# The Little Book of
# Shame

*What shame really means,
and how to shift from low self-esteem
to empowering self-acceptance*

Kristina Cizmar

"The Shame Lady"

Published by Emote Promotions, LLC, Boulder, Colorado

Cover design by Lisa Kerans
Cover painting by Knysh Ksenya
Author photo by Zoe Scott

"The Shame Lady," "Shame Translator," "Shame BITES,"
"Shameshifters," and the "emote" logo are trademarks of
Emote Promotions, LLC.

www.TheShameLady.com

The information contained in this book and supplemental
downloadable worksheet is for educational purposes only. The
author and publisher disclaim all liability that may arise as a
result of using this information. This book and supplemental
worksheet do not and cannot substitute for obtaining medical,
mental health, legal, or professional coaching advice, services, or
treatment from a qualified professional. References to external
sources are provided solely as a courtesy, and this book's author
and publisher do not have any control over and do not assume
any responsibility for their content.

ISBN: 0692408851
ISBN-13: 978-0692408858

With gratitude to the women and men who have
participated in my Shifting Shame workshops.

~

Hearing from you touches my heart
like nothing else in this world.

# CONTENTS

| | Acknowledgments | i |
|---|---|---|
| Chapter 1 | Shame, Self-Esteem, and Worthiness | 1 |
| Chapter 2 | What's Wrong with Defining Shame as "I Am Bad"? | 5 |
| Chapter 3 | Shame, Groups, and Our Need to Belong | 7 |
| Chapter 4 | Shame Redefined | 11 |
| Chapter 5 | Translating Our Shame | 15 |
| Chapter 6 | Shame BITES | 21 |
| Chapter 7 | Restoring Empowerment | 25 |
| Chapter 8 | Embodied Shame | 29 |
| Chapter 9 | Shame, Pride, and Humility | 33 |
| Appendix A | Charles M. Jones and the Jones Theory of Emotion | 37 |
| Appendix B | For Adult Survivors of Childhood Sexual Abuse | 39 |

# ACKNOWLEDGMENTS

This book would not exist without the brain of Charles M. Jones. Charles is a brilliant independent cognitive scientist who has dedicated his life to promoting humanity's adaptive interpretation of emotions. Over several years, I have had the privilege of spending many hours discussing cognition and emotions with Charles. As I became familiar with Charles' work on emotions, which at that point had been primarily used to shift anger, I sensed that his approach could be adapted to shifting shame – an emotion I had struggled with all my life.

I also owe a debt of gratitude to Jim Knickerbocker, coach, consultant, and extraordinary expert in workshop design. Jim, Charles, and I worked together to create an experiential workshop called "Shifting Shame," which has received rave reviews each time it's been delivered.

I'm very grateful to Florence Wetzel, my dear friend and editor, for making this book a smoother read. I'm all the more grateful that she made the time to do this while traveling in Sweden!

I'm extremely grateful to the very talented Lisa Kerans for designing a beautiful cover! Her patience and kindness are true blessings.

Tim Schultz built www.ShameTranslator.com, a web app that nicely complements this book. I'm very grateful for his dedication and patience in making it happen.

Last, but not least, I could not have written this without the support of my daughter, Zoe. Her name means "life" in Greek, and although I gave birth to her, it is Zoe who has given *me* the gift of life.

# CHAPTER 1

# SHAME, SELF-ESTEEM, AND WORTHINESS

There are a handful of ways in which we describe our feelings of basic inadequacy. We might say we feel shame; or we might have a sense that we have low self-worth or feel unworthy. We might think we aren't 'good enough'; or say that we have no sense of personal value. We might have "imposter syndrome" and fear being found out as not good enough to hold a position of responsibility. We might call it low self-esteem; or we may think we need to work on self-acceptance.

What each of these ways has in common is that they are all pointing to the feeling that we are inadequate as human beings. This feeling may be related to a particular action or accomplishment (or lack thereof), or it may not. In this book I'll use the word *shame* to refer to this entire constellation of ways that we experience badness, insufficiency, and valuelessness.

Aside from expressing the various forms of shame in words, we also express shame in at least two other ways, with or without the words attached. We express shame through our bodies and through our behavior.

Our bodies often show shame by shrinking, hiding, or covering up. We might hunch our shoulders, slouch, cross our arms in front of our chest, or even curl up in a ball. Our eyes might be cast downward, we might blush, or we might avoid eye contact. We might try to blend into the background, for fear of being seen, because we believe if someone were to truly see us, they would know we don't measure up.

Shame can also show up in our behavior, both through our actions or our inactions. The desire to fix the feeling can sometimes manifest as a drive to do more, and to be more. As with anything that falls out of balance, the imbalance can go in two opposite directions, and fall on a spectrum from too much to too little. So although shame can manifest as an endless drive, it can also manifest as doing nothing—a "why bother because I'll fail anyway" attitude. The same person can also manifest shame in different ways in different aspects of life, or at different times.

Shame often operates outside of awareness. It can have a real impact on our life even if we don't put any words to it.

The first step to solving any problem is to name the problem. Calling our problem *shame* is a great first step. Ironically, however, we may then experience more shame when we name our feeling *shame*! In other words, we feel ashamed of our shame. For some of us, the shame of naming the feeling *shame* may prevent us from ever taking the first step.

We might know intellectually that we have value just because we're human, but we can't talk ourselves out of our feelings because we think they aren't rational. Unfortunately, many approaches to working with shame try to do just that—they attempt to intellectually convince us that our shame is not a valid way to feel. They tell us we "should" accept ourselves as we are. This might offer a temporary fix for some of us, but it's not a lasting solution. It can lead to an endless cycle of feeling bad about oneself, then trying to talk oneself out of feeling bad, and then feeling worse when that doesn't work. This is a classic example of a *shame cycle*.

Once we take the first step of naming shame, we move on to further defining the problem.

# CHAPTER 2

# WHAT'S WRONG WITH DEFINING SHAME AS "I AM BAD"?

Sometimes our answers to questions are shaped by how we define the problem. We may unwittingly and unintentionally confine our possible solutions to one small box because of our language, assumptions, and past learning. Shame is one of those problems where our explanations—and therefore our solutions—have been confined to a small box by our language and thinking.

Anyone who has spent any amount of time reading about shame has probably heard that shame means "I am bad." At first, this seems to make a lot of sense, and it probably resonates with how we feel. Shame is different from guilt, which we're told means "I did something bad." When someone experiences shame about a particular action, it typically does seem deeper and more pervasive than guilt. In contrast to guilt, shame often feels as though it concerns our very nature.

However, there are three major problems with defining shame as "I am bad."

First, it's a dead end. If I am telling myself the story that I am bad—that there's something essentially wrong with who I am—then there isn't much I can do, since I can't change who I am. I can change my behavior, and I can perhaps change many things in my life, but I can't change who I essentially am. If I am bad, then there's nowhere to go.

Second, therapists know that globalizing negative thoughts is a hallmark of depression. This means thoughts such as:

- Nobody likes me
- I can never get out of bed
- Everything I do is a failure
- My life is a complete mess

Notice how "I am bad" fits very well alongside these kinds of global negative statements. Defining shame as "I am bad" inclines us toward depression.

Third, the "I am bad" definition of shame ignores the social context in which shame arises. Shame is not a feeling that arises in a vacuum. It is deeply rooted in our basic human need to belong.

# CHAPTER 3

# SHAME, GROUPS, AND
# OUR NEED TO BELONG

We all belong to many different groups. Some are based on location, such as:

- people shopping at a store at the same time as we are
- everyone living in our neighborhood
- members of our gym
- citizens of our particular country

Other groups might be based on our preferences or purchases, such as:

- people who love cheesecake
- Grateful Dead fans
- owners of a particular brand of laptop
- orange-beverage drinkers

We are members of groups based on our physical

characteristics or talents, such as:

- redheads
- brown-eyed women
- soccer players
- people who are supportive of others

We are also members of groups based on our family and interpersonal relationships, such as:

- ethnic group
- descendants of our great-grandmother
- immediate family
- intimate partnership

These are just a few of many possible examples of groups we may belong to. The categories presented above are not exhaustive, and they can overlap—such as redheads from England who like hot sauce.

A group may consist of many people, a few people, or even just two people, such as in a marriage or close friendship.

We humans are social animals. From the time when we are helpless infants throughout our entire adulthood, we rely on other people to survive and thrive. As the saying goes, no man is an island. Belonging to groups is an essential part of being human. From an evolutionary standpoint, belonging to groups is crucial to our survival, and therefore *it matters how we appear to other group members*.

That is where shame comes in. Shame can be a healthy emotion, keeping us in line with whatever values the group holds, which allows us to remain members in good standing. Even when there's no fear of punishment or retribution, we may do things (or refrain from doing things) simply to avoid feeling shame within a group.

For example, I might choose not to walk around my (very safe) neighborhood in my underwear because doing so would bring shame to myself (and my daughter by association!). I can imagine that if I were to do this, I might be shunned by my neighbors.

So, since I wish to remain a neighbor in good standing—in other words, a member of my neighborhood who is perceived as sensible and somewhat modest—I wear respectable clothing when I walk around my neighborhood. That is what I wish my identity within my neighborhood group to be, and having this identity will allow me to comfortably belong.

On the other hand, in the privacy of my own home, with the curtains drawn, I can walk around in my underwear and not feel shame. My family is used to seeing me this way and they accept me anyway, and my neighbors don't see me so they don't know (provided they don't read this book!).

So, within my neighborhood, shame is keeping me from doing something shameful, because I wish to personify the ideal of a sensible and modest neighbor within my neighborhood.

Within my family, on the other hand, I prefer to personify the ideal of a mother who is comfortable with her body and dresses comfortably at home.

Shame often works this way. There are certain things that we might feel ashamed of in one group, but not in another group.

**Reflection:**
What are some groups I belong to?

What is something I feel ashamed of in one group, but not in another?

# CHAPTER 4

## SHAME REDEFINED

How do we define shame in a way that is not a dead end, that isn't a globalized negative statement, and that takes our social setting into account?

We have a basic human need for autonomy, which means a need to direct our own selves. Being stuck in shame, in other words, means being stuck in an "I am bad" story. As a result we feel powerless, stripped of our sense of personal agency. That is a dead-end street, with nowhere to go.

We do have a tendency to overgeneralize our shame, interpreting it as "I am bad." We may *articulate* the feeling this way, or we may *embody* the feeling this way, or we may *act* out of this subconscious interpretation, perhaps without articulating it.

Yet shame is not just about who we are, so it can't possibly mean simply "I am bad." Shame is about who we are in the context of a given group. Shame is in the eye of the group. There are things we feel ashamed of in certain groups, but not in other groups.

When shame is turned inward, as epitomized by the

statement "I am bad," we are not acknowledging the relationship of shame to groups. Turning shame inward in this way is toxic.

On the other hand, shame that is addressed within the context of our roles in groups is a healthy force.

In the language of self-acceptance, when we focus on "self" we get stuck in the infamous shame cycle. When we focus on "acceptance" in our groups, we can escape the cycle and move forward.

In the language of not believing we're good enough, when we say "I'm not good enough" this means that we are at a dead end. When we complete the sentence and say what we really mean, which is "I'm not good enough *to belong*," we have options.

The most comprehensive definition of shame comes from cognitive scientist Charles M. Jones, whose radical (and radically simple) new theory of emotion tells us that emotions communicate our assessments of our own effectiveness.[1] Here's his definition of shame:

**Shame** arises
when I am **committed**
to personifying an **ideal**
for a **role** that I play
in a **group** I belong to
and I'm **failing** to do so.

We can see from this comprehensive definition that shame is less about our self and more about our basic need for acceptance.

The positive side of this definition of shame is that it is very specific. The definition helps us see doorways out of the pain of shame. These doorways have always been available to us, but they have been obscured by the

---

[1] See Appendix A for more information about the Jones Theory of Emotion.

blinders of "I am bad."

On the downside, this definition is a mouthful compared to the simplicity of "I am bad." But then again, recall that *all* of those globalized negatives that are hallmarks of depression have the same succinct appeal. For example, it's easier to say "I always fail" than it is to say "I fail under these specific conditions." But because the latter statement is more specific, it opens doors to possibilities that are not even visible in the shadow of "I always fail." Likewise, even though this new definition of shame is not succinct, it opens doors to possibilities that are not even visible in the shadow of "I am bad."

Since this new definition is extensive, I'll break down each line.

### **Shame** arises

Emotions always happen in the present moment. We may feel emotions about things that happened in the past, but our emotions are in the present. We may recall past emotions, and have a present emotional reaction that is the same or different from what we felt in the past. What we are looking at here is the present-moment emotion of shame when it arises within us.

### when I am **committed**

For shame to arise, we must be committed to the next three lines. If we aren't committed, then we won't care, and we won't feel shame.

### to personifying an **ideal**

An ideal is a standard of excellence. It can also be thought of as a standard of acceptability. It represents what one "should" be, "should" do, or "should" have in order to be accepted in a given group.

### for a **role** that I play

We all have multiple roles that we play in life, such as

mother, father, sister, brother, employee, consumer, traveler, student, reader, and so on.

### in a **group** I belong to

As discussed in chapter 3, we all belong to numerous groups. We may feel a certain kind of shame in one group, but not in another. We may also feel shame in the context of more than one group.

### and I'm **failing** to do so.

It is the failing that causes the shame to arise. If we were succeeding, we would feel pride.

# CHAPTER 5

## TRANSLATING OUR SHAME

How do we apply this definition of shame in our life? Because we are so accustomed to internalizing shame and thinking it's only about who we are, it takes practice to see shame through this new lens that takes our social embeddedness into account. We, in effect, need to translate our shame.

Here are some examples of shame, along with their translations. Notice that the same "stuck shame" could translate differently for different people, and it may also translate differently for the same person within different groups. I've included two possible translations for each example of stuck shame, but there could be many more.

Note that when translating your shame, it can be helpful to also make note of a group where you don't feel this shame, so I've included an example of this as well.

### Example 1
**Stuck shame:** I am ashamed that I go to therapy.
**Translation 1:** I am ashamed within my family because

family members should already be in good mental health.

**Translation 2:** I am ashamed at work because anyone who is an employee at my company should already be mentally stable.

**A group I don't feel this shame in:** I am not ashamed within my circle of close friends because in our group, members value personal growth and know that therapy is one possible pathway.

### Example 2

**Stuck shame:** I am ashamed that I was abused as a child and am just now dealing with it as an adult.

**Translation 1:** Within my intimate relationship, I am ashamed because a partner should have already "gotten over" their childhood.

**Translation 2:** I am ashamed within my family because family members should let bygones be bygones.

**A group I don't feel this shame in:** Within my abuse support group, I don't feel shame because all the members share a similar history, and we all know that people often do not work through childhood abuse until they are adults.

### Example 3

**Stuck shame:** I feel ashamed of my body.

**Translation 1:** I am ashamed at the gym, because people who work out there should already be in decent shape.

**Translation 2:** I am ashamed in my marriage because a wife should remain slender.

**A group I don't feel this shame in:** When I am with my book group, I don't feel shame because the highest value in this group is intellect, so body shape and athletic ability don't matter.

### Example 4

**Stuck shame:** I am ashamed that I don't earn a high income.

**Translation 1:** I am ashamed within my immediate family,

because for my family, being successful means earning a high salary.

**Translation 2:** I am ashamed at work because prestigious employees are ones who earn at least six figures.

**A group I don't feel this shame in:** Among the people who donate time or money to my local animal shelter, I feel proud that I can give something to a cause we all value.

### Example 5

**Stuck shame:** I am ashamed that I got a divorce.

**Translation 1:** I am ashamed within my extended family because to be a respected adult within my family, one must remain married for life.

**Translation 2:** I am ashamed within my spiritual community because congregation members should make their marriage work at all costs.

**A group I don't feel this shame in:** Within my closest friendships, we place a higher value on pursuit of happiness, so I feel proud that I took an important yet difficult step.

### Example 6

**Stuck shame:** I am ashamed that my father was an alcoholic.

**Translation 1:** I am ashamed within my family because loyal family members don't talk about this outside the family, and I have.

**Translation 2:** I am ashamed with my friends that I've had since childhood, because friends in this group should have had "normal" upbringings.

**A group I don't feel this shame in:** Within my support group, because this experience is one we all share.

### Example 7

**Stuck shame:** I am ashamed that I stay with a partner who treats me unkindly.

**Translation 1:** I am ashamed with my closest friends because someone in our friendship circle should demand better treatment from their partner.

**Translation 2:** I am ashamed with my family because someone in our family should know how to choose a good partner.

**A group I don't feel this shame in:** With a new therapist I can imagine having. (Recall that two people can constitute a group, and it may feel safest to start small.)

The "stuck shame" is the shame story we've fallen into. Usually this story is all about ourselves. The translated shame looks at which specific group we feel the shame in and why. The "why" needs to include the role we play in the group, as well as the ideal we're failing to live up to. The ideal is set by the group and applies to people who play this role within the group.

Here's another way to break down the translation. This format is known as the Shame Translator™.

Start by identifying something you feel shame around:

I am ashamed that I_____

_____.

Now tease apart this shame by filling in the blanks as indicated below. You may need to do this multiple times for each group you experience the shame in.

I am ashamed because

within  _____

[group I belong to]

anyone who plays the role of _____
                              [my role in the group]

"should" be
"should" have
or "should" behave in this way:

_____.
[the ideal: what is expected of someone in this role in this group].

Notice that the preceding examples follow this basic Shame Translator™ format.

To download a Shame Translator™ worksheet, visit www.TheShameLady.com/bookbonus.

If you're having trouble figuring out what group you feel ashamed in, it may be that every group you currently belong to is one in which you feel this shame. In that case, you may gain some perspective by imagining a group in which you *don't* feel this shame. Then go back and try once again to translate the shame, teasing it out in various groups you belong to.

If you're having trouble figuring out what ideal and which role you are feeling shame about (and there may be several), you can ask yourself "Who *doesn't* feel this shame?" and then "What's different about them?" Once you discover what the ideal is, return to the translation process.

If you are feeling shame around something that you did, something that you can never take back, you may be experiencing a combination of shame, guilt, and/or regret. It may be helpful to remind yourself that emotions are always in the present moment. The deed that triggers the emotions may have been in the past, but it is the emotion in the present that needs attention.

Shame, guilt, and regret can become entangled, but they are distinct emotions, each worthy of their own book.

Guilt is about violating an ethic, and it can be independent of belonging to any group. Guilt gets tied to shame because most groups hold the ideal that its members should be ethical. The purpose of regret is to prevent us from repeating the behavior that triggered it. If you are feeling guilt or regret, working with shame will be an important step, but you may need to work with these other emotions separately. In terms of shame, as we go forward in our life, we all have the ability to choose which ideals we'd like to try to personify.

What if we are feeling shame about something someone else did? We might hear, for example, that a family's "black sheep" brought shame upon the family. What does this really mean? What's happening is this: you, or at least some part of you, believe that your *association* with this person is putting you at risk of exclusion. The entire family may even be at risk of being excluded. Going back to my example in chapter 3, my daughter would feel ashamed if I were to walk around my neighborhood in my underwear. If I were shunned by my neighbors for doing this, there's a good chance she would be shunned as well. She can't change my behavior, but she can still use and benefit from the translation process. Using the Shame Translator™ helps to consciously define the situation, and uncover our underlying beliefs around it.

**Reflection:**
Practice translating shame for yourself using the Shame Translator™. To download a free Shame Translator™ worksheet, visit www.TheShameLady.com/bookbonus.

# CHAPTER 6

## SHAME BITES

Once someone translates their shame into this format, they can suddenly see possibilities that weren't previously visible to them. For example, they might examine one of the beliefs that they've uncovered, and decide they don't actually believe this. Or they may see that the importance of living up to this particular ideal is secondary to something else in their life. Or they may decide they *do* wish to live up to the ideal, and then find a new way to go about meeting the ideal. They may decide they want to change the way the group thinks about the ideal. They may even decide that they no longer wish to be a part of this group.

Notice that any one of these possibilities can lead to a shift out of the shame. Note also that each of these options is very different from the only option that was previously visible, namely trying to convince ourselves that we should simply not feel our shame.

These newly visible pathways out of shame fall into five categories. We can think of these pathways as Shame

BITES! Each letter of the BITES acronym stands for one area in which you might discover a way to shift out of your shame. You may wish to look at each of the five areas, or you may find that any one of the five on its own is all you need for the example of shame you're working with. Going through Shame BITES draws you into a process that allows you to adapt to your environment and circumstances. This in turn allows you to be more empowered and effective in your life.

**B is for Beliefs.** The process of translating our shame often reveals beliefs that were previously hidden. Once they are exposed, we can make conscious choices about whether we actually want to hold them or not. For example, I might decide that I don't really believe that people who go to my gym should *already* be in good shape.

**I is for Importance.** Once we expose the ideal that we've been failing to personify, we can make a conscious choice about what level of importance we want to give this ideal. We may decide that it is important to us, or we may decide that it actually is not as important as other priorities in our life. For example, I might see that I actually place a higher level of importance on spending time with my children than on having a large income.

**T is for Tactics.** If we have decided that this ideal is indeed one that we would like to embody, then we can look at what tactics or strategies might help us get there. For example, I might decide that long-term marriage is an ideal that I wish to uphold, and I may decide to suggest couples therapy as a strategy to prolong my marriage.

**E is for Environment**. Do we think this group should have this ideal? If not, do we want to commit to changing it, or contribute to changing it? Sometimes group ideals are like expired food in the back of the fridge: their time has passed, but they are still hanging around waiting for someone to point out that they need to be discarded. For example, I might decide that it doesn't make sense for adult survivors of childhood sexual abuse to have to heal "in the closet," and therefore I choose to work to make it more socially acceptable to heal "out loud."

**S is for Setting.** We may decide that we no longer wish to be a part of this group. In this case, we may look at what we will be gaining and what we will be giving up by leaving the group. For example, I might decide I want to leave my partner, even though that also means leaving a house I love.

Working with our translated shame in this way can help us see ways to shift out of shame, rather than staying stuck in it.

### Reflection:

What Shame BITES might I change?

# CHAPTER 7

# RESTORING EMPOWERMENT

Why is the motivation for our actions important? It matters because motivation determines how we'll feel in the process of taking the action, how likely we are to succeed, and how we feel after achieving the goal. The likelihood that we will achieve what we set out to do is impacted by what motivated us to set the goal in the first place.

Empowerment means doing something from our own power, rather than doing something because we should or must. In the first chapter, we looked at how we may resort to over-doing in order to compensate for low self-worth, often unconsciously. Doing from the energy of low self-worth leads to a feeling of emptiness. On the other hand, doing from our own sense of agency is empowering and fulfilling. The process in the preceding chapter helps move us from the old "I am bad" or "I am not enough" story into a sense of our own empowered ability to make a shift. It is this sense of agency and empowerment that is the true antidote to shame.

Because our old shame-stories have left so many of us feeling disempowered, this sense of power over our own selves, this sense of personal agency, is enormously healing. I have seen it transform people in front of my eyes.

Our life is made up of stories. The stories we tell ourselves have a way of shaping our life. If we are in a story that who we are is bad or not good enough, that is the story we live. When we shift our story—not from some artificially imposed directive (another shame-producing "should"), but from a felt sense that we have the power to choose differently—then we can live our life differently.

If we've lived the shame story long enough, we may find comfort there, because this shame story has become familiar. This blanket of shame offers some comfort and security, not only because it's what we've grown used to, but also because it helps us stay small. It keeps us hidden and sheltered, and it can be an excuse not to show our true selves.

Because of this tendency, it can be immensely helpful to find a "shame-shifting" buddy. Not because you should. Not because you are not good enough to do it on your own. Remember, the reason we do things—our motivation—matters. A shame-shifting buddy can be helpful because groups where we feel acceptance and support, even groups of just two people, are necessary in order to heal shame.

We have a basic human need to belong to groups. Shame, when it's working properly, helps us to meet this need. When it is misinterpreted and internalized, or ignored, it can lead to isolation and depression. We have the option of choosing to translate our shame, and finding a partner to join us in the journey. The very act of choosing and connecting with a partner can give us a first taste of this sense of agency and empowerment.

You may also visit the Shameshifters page at

www.shameshifters.net, or facebook.com/theshamelady to find our online community.

Other resources on shame note that shame seems to dissipate when it is shared with a friend or support group. This is often discussed as though it were some kind of miracle, something mysterious and unexplainable. But this is not a coincidence, and it is not a mystery. It is completely explainable. What's happening is this: in that moment of sharing what we are ashamed of with one or more people who instantly accept us anyway, a group is created where whatever it is we have been ashamed of is no longer shameful, and the act of sharing may even be a source of pride. We have an experience of acceptance, and this heals our shame because shame is our fear of not being good enough *to belong*. Whatever our shame was, we have a felt sense that we have transformed this shame into a force for connection, a way for us to *meet* our need to belong.

### Reflection:

What commitment do I genuinely want to make from my own heart, and not from any sense of "should"?

# CHAPTER 8

## EMBODIED SHAME

Shame is not just in our minds, it's also in our bodies. It might show up as scrunched-in shoulders, lowered chin, downcast eyes, avoidance of eye contact, flushed cheeks, arms crossed over the chest, or any other way of holding the body that shrinks or hides it. It may show up in our body as a felt sense of an internal roadblock, one that prevents us from allowing ourselves to be seen or heard. Embodied shame is a physical hiding of this thing that we perceive as being unacceptable to the group, and thus unacceptable to ourselves because, evolutionarily speaking, we need the group.

There are two important ways that we can use embodied shame to our advantage. First, it can help us to recognize when we are in a state of shame. Second, we can use our embodiment to help us shift out of shame.

We can increase our own awareness by asking ourselves, "How does shame show up for me in my body? What is my personal shame 'signature'?" Once we know this, we can start to pay attention to when our shame

29

signature arises, and this may be our first clue that we have slipped into shame. This is a really valuable tool because it's possible to be in a state of shame without having any conscious thoughts about it or without naming it. Paying attention to our embodied signs of shame can help us name it. In this way, our embodied shame becomes a tool for self-awareness, because we now have a cue that lets us know we have shame that we can work with.

In working with shame using the process in this book, embodied shame automatically starts to shift for many people. We feel the shame arise in our body, we breathe into it, we acknowledge it. Then we make the effort to translate it so that we can see what it is that is interfering with our ability to belong. By doing this, we generate options for resolving the shame. This process often produces a noticeable bodily shift. We may stand up taller, raise our chin, or look people in the eye. The sense of empowerment we start to feel is not just in our minds, it's also in our bodies.

So far we have talked about shifting our shame by working directly with the trigger for the emotion. For those of us who have experienced chronic shame—where shame has become our normal state—it can be very challenging to let go of. It's like a heavy coat that is hard to take off because we have become accustomed to its presence. It may be a comforting burden in some ways because it allows us to remain small and unseen.

Because shame can be so entrenched, it helps to reinforce this work in another way. Consider this: how we feel influences how we hold our bodies. The opposite, however, is also true. How we hold our bodies influences how we feel. We feel happy, so we smile. But if we smile, it can actually lead to feeling happier.

So how do we embody worthiness? There is actually research that shows that standing in a power pose for two minutes in a shame-free private space leads to feeling more powerful, more self-confident, and more worthy of taking up space. Amy Cuddy shares two of these power poses in her 2012 TEDTalk.[2]

One is the Wonder Woman pose: standing tall, feet slightly wider than your hips, hands on your hips, chest and chin up. Another is the universal victory pose: standing up straight, arms reached above your head in a V, chin up.

We can also borrow a practice from somatic attachment expert Diane Poole Heller.[3] Avoiding eye contact is one hallmark of shame, and interestingly it's also a hallmark of what's called avoidant attachment. One amazingly powerful way to work with this is the "kind eyes" exercise, where we practice connecting through eye contact. Find a photo of a person with kind eyes, who has a gentle gaze forward. It doesn't need to be someone you know. Spend a few minutes allowing yourself to rest into their gaze. Notice what this brings up for you.

These practices where we increase our awareness of shame in our body, and where we embody our own worthiness, can help sustain our shift out of shame. We literally become grounded in our own self-worth.

### Reflection:

How does shame show up in my body? What is my body's shame signature?

Can I visualize myself as no longer wearing the heavy coat of shame?

If I spend two minutes in a power pose every day for a week, what do I notice?

---

[2] See www.ted.com/talks/amy_cuddy_your_body_language_shapes_who_you_are

[3] For more on Diane Poole Heller's work, visit dianepooleheller.com

# CHAPTER 9

# SHAME, PRIDE, AND HUMILITY

We have a basic human need to belong to groups. Shame arises as a result of our fear of being excluded from groups. It is a feeling of not being worthy of belonging. From birth through adulthood, our well-being depends upon our connections with other people. Our need to belong is so great that being excluded from a group can even be experienced as a trauma in and of itself. Shame, at its best, helps us to meet our need to belong by guiding us toward behaviors that are in line with the ideals of the groups we belong to, so that we may try to avoid the pain (and other potential detrimental outcomes) of exclusion.

As a society, we *want* people to be ashamed of certain things that we deem unacceptable, such as theft or violent crime. Shame is what gives us morality even in the absence of shared spiritual or religious beliefs. Shame helps us cohabitate.

We've seen that shame turned inward is toxic, whereas shame that is addressed within the context of our roles in groups is a healthy force.

Now let's turn our attention to pride. In chapter 4 we noted that if we *succeed* at personifying an ideal for our role in our group, we feel pride. In this way, pride is the opposite of shame. Pride, like shame, can function in a toxic way or a healthy way. Toxic pride looks like arrogance, an attitude of "I'm too good to belong." On the other hand, pride experienced with awareness of our role in our group can have the effect of raising the standards of the group. An example would be a proud athlete setting a new world record. Or human-rights advocates setting a new standard of acceptability for treatment of women in a particular country.

In chapter 1, we talked about how being out of balance in any realm can mean one of two extremes. If we imagine a spectrum with extreme shame ("I am not good enough to belong") on one side, and extreme pride ("I am too good to belong") on the other side, the midpoint between these two extremes would represent balance. Humility is the middle ground between shame and pride. Humility is a state of believing we are on par with others.

Humility, like shame, is often misinterpreted. Some conceptions of humility include lowering one's own worth in comparison to others, but this is not true humility. So what is humility? Humility is a recognition of our own intrinsic self-worth, and also seeing this same intrinsic self-worth in others. It's a setting aside of comparisons and judgments, and instead honoring ourselves and others as we are. True humility is a "heartset," which is something far more pervasive than a mindset. Not only is humility a way of relating to others that invites connection, it is also a way of staying grounded in ourselves, and a way of showing up in the world with greater aliveness and presence. (In my workshops, I call this "Living life in CAPs—with Connection, Aliveness, and Presence.")

Being in humility is like flowing easefully down a river. On one bank we have shame, on the other pride. Shame is a powerful force for keeping us in the flow of humility. Shame at its best helps keep us in easeful presence and connection with other people. It encourages self-control and conduct that is in alignment with our group's ideals. Pride is a force for *upgrading* our group's ideals.

When shame is misinterpreted as some version of "I am bad" and removed from the social context in which it arises, it becomes self-destructive—an inward-facing dagger. Translating our shame back into the social context restores shame to its rightful place as a force for keeping us in a state of flow, for keeping us in the river of humility.

# APPENDIX A

## CHARLES M. JONES AND
## THE JONES THEORY OF EMOTION

The Jones Theory of Emotion states that:
Emotions arise in response to our subconscious assessments that we *are* or *are not* on track to fulfill a need that is in play.

- Pleasurable emotions arise when our subconscious has the assessment that we *are* on track to fulfill a need.
- Painful emotions arise when our subconscious has the assessment that we *are not* on track to fulfill a need.

According to this new theory, painful emotions are important messages. They call on us to look at something, and make a change that will lead us to be more effective in our life.

For each of our emotions, such as anger, shame, and guilt, Charles M. Jones offers a new definition of the emotion. These new definitions are not simply a reframing.

They are insightful interpretations based on his revolutionary theory of emotional causation.

This is his definition of shame, which appears in chapter 4 of this book:

Shame arises
when I am committed
to personifying an ideal
for a role that I play
in a group I belong to
and I'm failing to do so.

The BITES process for working with shame was developed in consultation with Charles M. Jones.

To learn more about the work of Charles M. Jones, visit the Institute for Adaptive Mastery at www.adaptivemastery.com.

# APPENDIX B

# FOR ADULT SURVIVORS OF CHILDHOOD SEXUAL ABUSE

One of the toughest types of shame to shake is the shame of being sexually abused as a child. It's often expressed as some form of "I am dirty." This is the type of dirtiness that no amount of bathing or scrubbing can wash off. Sadly, many of us experience this form of shame even before we can speak the word or understand the concept.

In my own experience of this shame, I know that even as a child without the words for it, I picked up on my abuser's shame. His verbal and nonverbal communication told me that what he was doing was shameful. The behavior involved me, therefore the shame was mine too, by association. It became a secret—something that could never be shared, or else I would surely be abandoned by the various groups I relied on as a child (family, school, friends, etc.). I did not have those thoughts consciously. It was as though the innate need to belong (and thus survive) silently led this process.

It can be challenging to translate this deep level of shame by using the process in this book, but *it is possible*. If you are struggling with this, here are just two examples of what the Shame Translator™ might look like. Be aware that this process can look very different for different people. One person might need to fill this out in many different ways in order to address the different facets of this complex shame.[4]

### Example 1
I am ashamed because
within <u>my town</u> [group I belong to]
anyone who plays the role of <u>a child</u> [my role in the group] "should" be / "should" have / or "should" behave in this way: <u>should be pure and innocent.</u> [the ideal: what is expected of someone in this role in this group]

Using Shame BITES from chapter 6, I might then examine my **B**eliefs around what makes a child "pure and innocent." Or I might see that I place more **I**mportance on the responsibility of those in a caregiver role who "should" protect rather than harm children.

### Example 2
I am ashamed because
within <u>my family</u> [group I belong to]
anyone who plays the role of <u>an abused child</u> [my role in the group]
"should" be / "should" have / or "should" behave in this way: <u>should not do anything to initiate abuse</u> [the ideal: what is expected of someone in this role in this group].

It's not uncommon to feel as though something about us or something we did makes us responsible for the fact that the abuse happened. Turning to Shame BITES, I examine my **B**eliefs. Thinking of a particular time when I believe

---

[4] Childhood sexual abuse often results in what's known as *complex trauma*. It's accompanied by what could be termed *complex shame*.

that something I did initiated an instance of abuse, I recall that when there is a relationship with an imbalance of power, the onus is *always* on the person with greater power to do the right thing. This principle has been upheld in cases of teacher-student and doctor-patient relationships, even where both parties are *adults*, so this most definitely applies to caregiver-child relationships. Realizing this, I am able to shift out of this portion of my shame.

Notice that I can choose to go through each element of BITES, or I may find that one or two are enough to give me the shift that I'm looking for. I experience the shift as a feeling of tension releasing in my body.

For help with beliefs around abuse, www.TenKeys.org is an excellent resource.

# ABOUT THE AUTHOR

Kristina Cizmar is affectionately known as "The Shame Lady." She considers her life to be a study in shame. Like one in five women and one in thirteen men across the globe, Kristina is a survivor of childhood sexual abuse. It has been her own healing journey that brought her to this work.

In 2014, Kristina launched TenKeys.org, which presents a holistic approach to healing from childhood sexual abuse. The Ten Keys are a framework for healing that arose from Kristina's extensive research, personal experience, and interactions with other survivors.

While working on the Ten Keys approach to healing, she realized that shame is one of the deepest parts of this childhood wound, and also one of the most challenging aspects of healing. There is the shame of the initial abuse, and another hit of shame around the healing process.

After trying various ways of working with shame, self-esteem, personal value, and self-acceptance, she discovered the core reason why nothing led her to a permanent shift. And then she developed an approach that not only created a shift for herself, but has been helping others do the same.

Kristina offers interactive workshops as well as a keynote presentation on "Shifting Shame," which she presents to a wide range of audiences including fellow abuse survivors, the LGBTQ community, universities, and workplaces. If you are interested in bringing one of these offerings to your organization or conference, write theshamelady@gmail.com.

Kristina resides in Boulder, Colorado with her daughter, Zoe. She has called Oregon, Ohio, Florida, Rhode Island, and New York home.

# CONNECT WITH KRISTINA

www.TheShameLady.com
www.Facebook.com/TheShameLady
twitter: @theshamelady

To download your free copy of the Shame Translator™
worksheet used in chapter 5, visit
www.TheShameLady.com/bookbonus